Sisters' Journal

Sisters' Journal

STORIES, REFLECTIONS, AND CHERISHED KEEPSAKES

L.J. Tracosas

Bluestreak
BOOKS

For my sister, Willa, for inspiring me
and for all the chick-flick recs.

Love you too, too much.

Weldon Owen International
1045 Sansome Street, Suite 100, San Francisco, CA 94111
www.weldonowen.com

Edited and designed by Girl Friday Productions
www.girlfridayproductions.com

Library of Congress Cataloging in Publication data is available.

ISBN: 978-168188-464-6

First Printed in 2019
10 9 8 7 6 5 4 3 2 1
2019 2020 2021 2022

Printed and bound in China

Illustration Credits:
©Shutterstock/Irtsya: cover; ©Shutterstock/Maria_Galybina: cover; ©Shutterstock/Viktoriya Yakubouskaya: cover, endsheets; ©Shutterstock/lena_nikolaeva: pocket, 2, 3, 46, 47, 94, 95; ©Shutterstock/Yamurchik: 4, 5, 6, 7, 8–9, 14, 15, 20, 21, 34, 35, 76, 77; ©Shutterstock/Nadia Grapes: 10–11, 12, 13, 92, 93; ©Shutterstock/Alenka Karabanova: 16, 17, 82, 83; ©Shutterstock/Ola_S: 18, 19; ©Shutterstock/Larissa-S: 22, 23; ©Shutterstock/Tata_ota: 24, 25, 84, 85; ©Shutterstock/JuliyaM: 26, 27; ©Shutterstock/helterskelter: 28, 29, 74, 75; ©Shutterstock/Helga Gavrilova: 30, 31; ©Shutterstock/blossomstar: 32, 33; ©Shutterstock/berry2046: 36, 37; ©Shutterstock/logaryphmic: 38, 39; ©Shutterstock/KateChe: 40, 41; ©Shutterstock/Ksenia Lokko: 42, 43, 56, 57, 80, 81; ©Shutterstock/Angelina Bambina: 44, 45, 66, 67; ©Shutterstock/EkaterinaP: 48–49; ©Shutterstock/subbery: 50, 51; ©Shutterstock/Elena Melnikova: 52, 53; ©Shutterstock/kidstudio852: 54, 55; ©Shutterstock/Angyee Patipat: 58, 59; ©Shutterstock/Lavrushka: 60, 61; ©Shutterstock/Iveta Angelova: 62, 63; ©Shutterstock/Olga Rom: 64, 65; ©Shutterstock/sunniwa: 68, 69; ©Shutterstock/Tanya Syrytsyna: 70, 71, 72–73; ©Shutterstock/Lera Efremova: 78, 79; ©Shutterstock/solmariart: 86–87; ©Shutterstock/Artnis: 88, 89; ©Shutterstock/Annykos: 90, 91; ©Shutterstock/Eireen Z: 96

This book is dedicated to

_____

_____

_____

_____

Contents

How to use this book

Throughout this journal, you'll find prompts that will help you explore your relationship as sisters, as well as your past, your present, and your future together. You and your sister will each complete your own profiles at the start of the book, with one of you choosing the I AM section (in teal) and the other filling out the YOU ARE section (in pink). Throughout these pages you'll each answer prompts depending on your profile. For some prompts, you'll want to brainstorm together with your sister and fill in what you've come up with. You can complete the book either by passing it back and forth or by interviewing each other. The goal is to share and communicate with each other, and to record your thoughts, feelings, and memories together.

Some pages include photo frames, where you can add your own photos using photo corners or other photo-safe scrapbooking supplies. If you don't have a photo, use the space to write a vivid description or to sketch a picture of the moment. At the back of the book, you'll find an envelope where you can keep more photos, cards, notes, and other keepsake memories from your sisterhood, and preserve them for years to come.

INTRODUCTION

Is solace anywhere more comforting
than in the arms of a sister?

—Alice Walker

Sisterhood—is there a relationship deeper, lovelier, or more complex? You and your sister share a childhood, but from different perspectives. You share clothes and books and ideas and secrets, but experience life as individuals. No one can get under your skin more than your sister, yet no one will have your back like her, either. Your sister feels your pain, and your joy too. You know her better than anyone, but she can still surprise you every day. You care about each other, fight with each other, protect each other, challenge each other. You can make each other cry, and you can make each other *laugh* till you cry.

Every pair of sisters is as unique as you both are individually. In these pages, explore your relationship— who you are, where you come from, and where you're going together. Your connection is strong and lifelong. Honor your bond here.

PART ONE

Who We Are

I AM . . .

*In the prompts throughout this book,
fill in the spaces labeled MY RESPONSE.
These are color-coded in teal.*

My full name is: _____

But you call me: _____

_____

I was born on: _____

I am your older / younger sister by: _____
        (Circle one.)

Right now, I live: _____

_____

_____

_____

_____

My first memory of you is: _____

_____

_____

_____

_____

_____

_____

_____

Here's a picture of when we met:

YOU ARE . . .

*In the prompts throughout this book,
fill in the spaces labeled YOUR RESPONSE.
These are color-coded in pink.*

My full name is: _____

But you call me: _____

_____

_____

I was born on: _____

I am your older / younger sister by: _____
      (Circle one.)

Right now, I live: _____

_____

_____

_____

_____

_____

My first memory of you is: _____

_____

_____

_____

_____

_____

_____

_____

Here's one of my favorite photos of when we were young:

WE ARE . . .

A sister is both your mirror—and your opposite.

—Elizabeth Fishel

Our relationship is like:

MY RESPONSE

_____

_____

_____

YOUR RESPONSE _____

_____

_____

_____

Describe me in one word.

MY RESPONSE _____

YOUR RESPONSE _____

Here are some words that describe your sister:

MY RESPONSE _____

_____

_____

_____

_____

YOUR RESPONSE _____

_____

_____

_____

_____

Your sister's best qualities are:

MY RESPONSE _____

_____

_____

_____

_____

_____

YOUR RESPONSE _____

_____

_____

_____

_____

Our parents would describe us as:

MY RESPONSE _____

_____

_____

_____

YOUR RESPONSE _____

_____

_____

_____

Other people would describe us as:

MY RESPONSE _____

_____

_____

_____

YOUR RESPONSE _____

_____

_____

_____

How are we the same?

MY RESPONSE _____

_____

_____

_____

YOUR RESPONSE _____

_____

_____

_____

How are we different?

MY RESPONSE _____

_____

_____

_____

YOUR RESPONSE _____

_____

_____

_____

One of my favorite memories from when we were growing up is:

MY RESPONSE _____

_____

_____

_____

_____

_____

_____

_____

_____

YOUR RESPONSE _____

_____

_____

_____

_____

_____

_____

_____

_____

One of the times we laughed the hardest was:

MY RESPONSE _____

_____

_____

YOUR RESPONSE _____

_____

_____

This is an event that sparked a running joke or ridiculous

nickname that still makes us laugh to this day:

MY RESPONSE _____

Running joke or nickname: _____

What happened: _____

_____

_____

_____

YOUR RESPONSE _____

Running joke or nickname: _____

What happened: _____

_____

_____

_____

One of the most difficult times we've been through together was:

MY RESPONSE _____

_____

_____

_____

_____

YOUR RESPONSE _____

_____

_____

_____

This is something I had to do alone, but I always wish

you could have been there with me:

MY RESPONSE _____

_____

_____

_____

YOUR RESPONSE _____

_____

_____

_____

The time in my life when I needed you the most was:

MY RESPONSE _____

_____

_____

_____

YOUR RESPONSE _____

_____

_____

_____

And you were there for me by:

MY RESPONSE _____

_____

_____

_____

_____

YOUR RESPONSE _____

_____

_____

_____

Shhh! This is a secret we kept between ourselves:

MY RESPONSE _____

_____

_____

_____

YOUR RESPONSE _____

_____

_____

_____

_____

I need to come clean: This is something I talked to our parents or other siblings

about behind your back.

MY RESPONSE _____

_____

_____

_____

YOUR RESPONSE _____

_____

_____

_____

_____

We got into the most trouble with our parents when:

MY RESPONSE _____

_____

_____

YOUR RESPONSE _____

_____

_____

What were the repercussions?

MY RESPONSE _____

_____

_____

YOUR RESPONSE _____

_____

_____

This is one time I totally covered for you or had your back when you were in trouble.

You owe me one!

MY RESPONSE _____

_____

_____

YOUR RESPONSE _____

_____

_____

When you're upset, you:

MY RESPONSE _____

_____

_____

YOUR RESPONSE _____

_____

_____

I try to help by:

MY RESPONSE _____

_____

_____

YOUR RESPONSE _____

_____

_____

The biggest fight we've ever gotten into was:

MY RESPONSE _____

_____

_____

_____

YOUR RESPONSE _____

_____

_____

_____

This is how we got over that fight, and what we learned from it:

MY RESPONSE _____

_____

_____

_____

_____

YOUR RESPONSE _____

_____

_____

_____

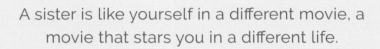

> A sister is like yourself in a different movie, a
> movie that stars you in a different life.
>
> —Deborah Tannen

The sisters in a movie, book, or TV show who are most like us are:

MY RESPONSE _____

_____

_____

YOUR RESPONSE _____

_____

_____

Because:

MY RESPONSE _____

_____

_____

YOUR RESPONSE _____

_____

_____

If our lives were a movie, it would be this genre:

MY RESPONSE _____

because _____

_____

YOUR RESPONSE _____

because _____

_____

The actor who would play you would be:

MY RESPONSE _____

because _____

_____

YOUR RESPONSE _____

because _____

_____

The actor who would play me would be:

MY RESPONSE _____

because _____

_____

YOUR RESPONSE _____

because _____

_____

The movie's title would be:

MY RESPONSE _____

YOUR RESPONSE _____

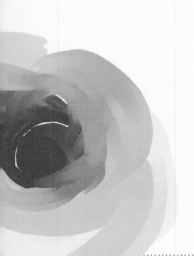

HOW WE CONNECT

WE STAY IN TOUCH . . .

(Circle one for each row)

BY TEXTING:	almost nonstop	at least once a day to see how you're doing	once in a while	I don't text
ON SOCIAL MEDIA:	all the time, about everything	I look at your feed sometimes	I wouldn't know what you are up to without it	I don't have an account
BY PHONE:	every day	every week	once in a while	just text me!

Other creative ways we do connect or could connect: _____

_____

Do we talk to each other enough, not enough, or too much? _____

_____

If not enough: How can we connect more? _____

_____

The topics we talk about most are:

MY RESPONSE _____

_____

_____

_____

_____

YOUR RESPONSE _____

_____

_____

_____

_____

The topics we don't love talking about are:

MY RESPONSE _____

_____

_____

_____

YOUR RESPONSE _____

_____

_____

_____

I always call you when I'm feeling:

MY RESPONSE _____

_____

_____

YOUR RESPONSE _____

_____

_____

I'll never forget when I got this phone call from you:

MY RESPONSE _____

_____

_____

_____

YOUR RESPONSE _____

_____

_____

_____

The hardest conversation we've ever had was:

MY RESPONSE _____

_____

_____

YOUR RESPONSE _____

_____

_____

The most exciting conversations we've ever had were about:

MY RESPONSE _____

_____

_____

_____

YOUR RESPONSE _____

_____

_____

_____

Add or describe a favorite piece of snail mail you've exchanged here,

such as a greeting card, letter, note, or postcard:

HANGING OUT

My sister and I truly are best friends.

—Solange Knowles

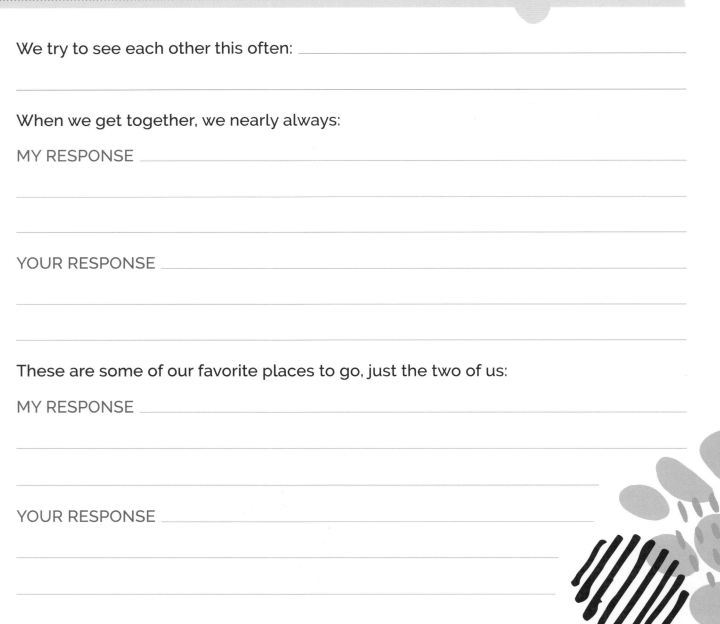

We try to see each other this often: _____

_____

When we get together, we nearly always:

MY RESPONSE _____

_____

_____

YOUR RESPONSE _____

_____

_____

These are some of our favorite places to go, just the two of us:

MY RESPONSE _____

_____

_____

YOUR RESPONSE _____

_____

Our idea of a perfect night in together is:

MY RESPONSE _____

_____

_____

_____

YOUR RESPONSE _____

_____

_____

_____

Something we used to do that we haven't done in a while is:

MY RESPONSE _____

_____

_____

_____

YOUR RESPONSE _____

_____

_____

_____

My favorite thing to do with you is:

MY RESPONSE _____

_____

_____

_____

YOUR RESPONSE _____

_____

_____

A FEW OF OUR FAVORITE THINGS

Here are a few lists of what we love.

COLOR

MY RESPONSE _____   YOUR RESPONSE _____

TIME OF YEAR

MY RESPONSE _____   YOUR RESPONSE _____

BOOKS

1. _____   1. _____

2. _____   2. _____

3. _____   3. _____

TV SHOWS

1. _____   1. _____

2. _____   2. _____

3. _____   3. _____

MOVIES

1. _____   1. _____

2. _____   2. _____

3. _____   3. _____

ACTORS

1. _____   1. _____

2. _____   2. _____

3. _____   3. _____

MUSIC BANDS / VOCALISTS

1. _____   1. _____

2. _____   2. _____

3. _____   3. _____

SONGS

1. _____   1. _____

2. _____   2. _____

3. _____   3. _____

GAMES

1. _____   1. _____

2. _____   2. _____

3. _____   3. _____

PLACES IN THE WORLD

1. _____   1. _____

2. _____   2. _____

3. _____   3. _____

CRUSHES, PAST OR PRESENT

1. _____   1. _____

2. _____   2. _____

3. _____   3. _____

GUILTY PLEASURES

Time to fess up: Here are some of our guilty pleasures.
Do *not* tell anyone!

A totally terrible movie that I absolutely love is:

MY RESPONSE _____

YOUR RESPONSE _____

I can't help but watch it, and you should too because:

MY RESPONSE _____

_____

YOUR RESPONSE _____

_____

Please do not tell anyone that I binge-watched this TV show:

MY RESPONSE _____

YOUR RESPONSE _____

I can't help but love it, and you should too because:

MY RESPONSE _____

_____

YOUR RESPONSE _____

_____

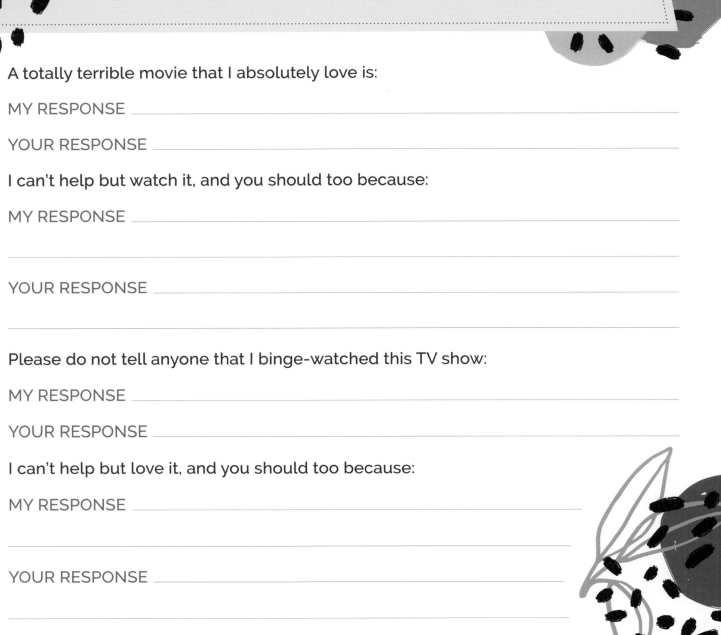

A song that I'm embarrassed to know all the words to is:

MY RESPONSE _____

YOUR RESPONSE _____

We would "dance like no one is watching" to these tunes:

1. _____

2. _____

3. _____

Do not tell anyone that I read this magazine sometimes:

MY RESPONSE _____

YOUR RESPONSE _____

I can't help but watch these videos on YouTube:

MY RESPONSE _____

_____

YOUR RESPONSE _____

_____

The star I follow on social media that I hope no one can see in my follow list is:

MY RESPONSE _____

YOUR RESPONSE _____

This is one more totally embarrassing thing that you know
about me—and that no one else does (please keep it that way):

MY RESPONSE _____

_____

YOUR RESPONSE _____

_____

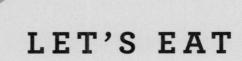

LET'S EAT

I always feel I'm writing more for you than for anybody.

—Virginia Woolf (in response to her sister Vanessa's
praise for her novel *The Waves*)

My top three desert-island foods—the foods that I can't live without—are:

MY RESPONSE

1. _____

2. _____

3. _____

YOUR RESPONSE

1. _____

2. _____

3. _____

I can't believe you don't like to eat:

MY RESPONSE _____

_____

YOUR RESPONSE _____

_____

Our favorite restaurants are:

1. _____

2. _____

3. _____

4. _____

5. _____

If I'm going to make you dinner, here's the recipe for something

I'd make that I think you would *love*:

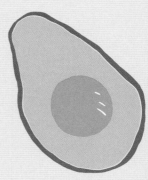

MY RESPONSE

Ingredients _____

_____

_____

Instructions _____

_____

_____

_____

_____

_____

_____

YOUR RESPONSE

Ingredients _____

_____

_____

Instructions _____

_____

_____

_____

_____

The home-cooked meal that we both loved the most when we were growing up is:

_____

Made by: _____

_____

We usually ate it: _____

_____

_____

HERE'S THE RECIPE:

Ingredients: _____

_____

_____

_____

Instructions: _____

_____

_____

_____

_____

_____

_____

_____

_____

_____

_____

The dessert that we had on special occasions when we were growing up is:

_____

Made by: _____

_____

We had it on these special occasions: _____

_____

HERE'S THE RECIPE:

Ingredients: _____

_____

_____

_____

Instructions: _____

_____

_____

_____

_____

_____

_____

_____

_____

_____

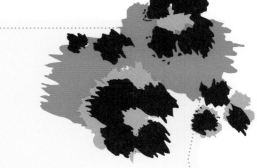

STYLE

Fashion fades, only style remains the same.

—Coco Chanel

I would describe your style as:

MY RESPONSE _____

_____

YOUR RESPONSE _____

_____

My favorite outfit you wear is:

MY RESPONSE _____

_____

YOUR RESPONSE _____

_____

My favorite piece of clothing you've lent me or given to me is:

MY RESPONSE _____

_____

YOUR RESPONSE _____

_____

My favorite accessory you wear is:

MY RESPONSE _____

_____

YOUR RESPONSE _____

_____

A style I think you should try is:

MY RESPONSE _____

_____

YOUR RESPONSE _____

_____

We clean up nice! I remember how stunning you looked when you dressed up in this

for a special occasion:

MY RESPONSE _____

Event: _____

Description of your sister: _____

_____

YOUR RESPONSE _____

Event: _____

Description of your sister: _____

_____

OK. I didn't tell you then, but the most ridiculous look you tried growing up was:

MY RESPONSE _____

_____

YOUR RESPONSE _____

THANK YOU

My predominant feeling is one of gratitude.
I have loved and been loved; I have been given much
and I have given something in return . . .

—Oliver Sacks

Thank you for teaching me . . .

MY RESPONSE _____

_____

_____

_____

_____

YOUR RESPONSE _____

_____

_____

_____

_____

Thank you for talking me out of . . .

MY RESPONSE _____

_____

_____

_____

YOUR RESPONSE _____

_____

_____

_____

Thank you for saving the day when . . .

MY RESPONSE _____

_____

_____

_____

_____

YOUR RESPONSE _____

_____

_____

PART TWO

Where We Come From

OUR FAMILY

Family is the most important thing in the world.

—Princess Diana

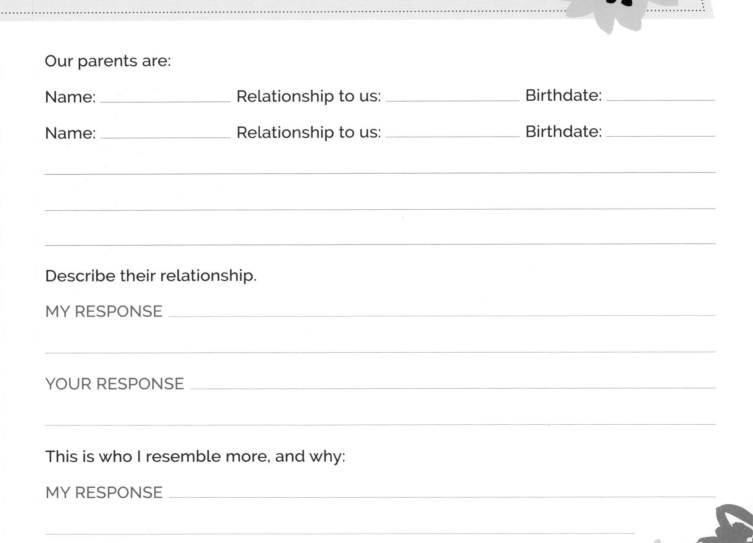

Our parents are:

Name: _____ Relationship to us: _____ Birthdate: _____

Name: _____ Relationship to us: _____ Birthdate: _____

_____

_____

_____

Describe their relationship.

MY RESPONSE _____

_____

YOUR RESPONSE _____

_____

This is who I resemble more, and why:

MY RESPONSE _____

_____

YOUR RESPONSE _____

_____

This is who you resemble more, and why:

MY RESPONSE _____

_____

YOUR RESPONSE _____

_____

Add a photo or write down a favorite memory we have with our parents.

_____

_____

_____

_____

_____

OUR EXTENDED FAMILY

These are important people in our extended family.

Name:	Relationship:	Three words to describe this person are:

Add a photo of or describe a big family gathering. _____

_____

_____

_____

_____

_____

_____

_____

_____

OTHER SISTERS IN OUR EXTENDED FAMILY

The words "we are sisters" went straight to her heart and nestled there.

—Louisa May Alcott

GRANDMOTHERS AND GREAT-AUNTS, MOTHERS AND AUNTS, EVEN CLOSE FAMILY FRIENDS: SISTERS INSPIRE SISTERS. HERE ARE SOME OF THE SISTER RELATIONSHIPS WE ADMIRE, OR DON'T WANT TO EMULATE, IN OUR EXTENDED FAMILY.

Names: _____ & _____

Who they are to us: _____

_____

Describe their relationship in a few words:

MY RESPONSE _____

YOUR RESPONSE _____

What we learned from them:

MY RESPONSE _____

_____

YOUR RESPONSE _____

_____

Names: _____ & _____

Who they are to us: _____

_____

Describe their relationship in a few words:

MY RESPONSE _____

YOUR RESPONSE _____

What we learned from them:

MY RESPONSE _____

_____

YOUR RESPONSE _____

_____

We love our family because: _____

_____

_____

These are the good qualities we learned from our family, and who we get them from:

MY RESPONSE   YOUR RESPONSE

1. _____   1. _____

2. _____   2. _____

3. _____   3. _____

These are some bad qualities we picked up from our family, and who we get them from:

MY RESPONSE   YOUR RESPONSE

1. _____   1. _____

2. _____   2. _____

3. _____   3. _____

OTHER IMPORTANT PEOPLE IN OUR LIVES

FAMILY IS HOW YOU DEFINE IT. SIGNIFICANT OTHERS, BEST FRIENDS, IMPORTANT NEIGHBORS, EVEN PETS AS FUZZY FAMILY MEMBERS—HERE ARE SOME OF THE IMPORTANT FIGURES IN OUR LIVES. WE'RE NOT RELATED BUT WE CONSIDER THEM FAMILY.

Name: _____ Relationship: _____

Describe them in three words: _____

Why this person is important to us: _____

_____

_____

Name: _____ Relationship: _____

Describe them in three words: _____

Why this person is important to us: _____

_____

_____

Name: _____ Relationship: _____

Describe them in three words: _____

Why this person is important to us: _____

_____

_____

_____

Name: _____ Relationship: _____

Describe them in three words: _____

Why this person is important to us: _____

_____

_____

_____

Name: _____ Relationship: _____

Describe them in three words: _____

Why this person is important to us: _____

_____

_____

_____

Name: _____ Relationship: _____

Describe them in three words: _____

Why this person is important to us: _____

_____

_____

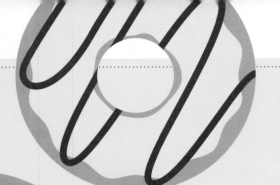

TRADITIONS

TRADITIONS ARE THE RITUALS WE CARRY ON THROUGH GENERATIONS. THEY CAN BE RELIGIOUS OR CULTURAL, THEY CAN MARK SPECIAL OCCASIONS, OR THEY CAN EVEN BE SMALL, EVERYDAY GESTURES THAT FAMILY MEMBERS DO FOR EACH OTHER. EXPLORE YOUR FAMILY TRADITIONS, OLD AND NEW, WHAT YOU'LL CARRY FORWARD, AND WHAT YOU MIGHT LEAVE BEHIND.

These are some of the traditions our family takes part in: _____

_____

_____

When we celebrate a birth or birthdays, we always do this: _____

_____

_____

We use these traditions to remember loved ones we've lost: _____

_____

_____

These are the traditions I plan to carry forward with my family and future generations:

MY RESPONSE _____

_____

_____

YOUR RESPONSE _____

_____

_____

I probably won't continue these traditions:

MY RESPONSE _____

_____

_____

YOUR RESPONSE _____

_____

_____

Add a photo that shows your family taking part in an important tradition.

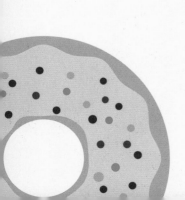

WHERE WE GREW UP

We spent most of our childhood at this address: _____

_____

Describe your childhood home:

MY RESPONSE _____

_____

_____

YOUR RESPONSE _____

_____

_____

Describe your hometown:

MY RESPONSE _____

_____

_____

YOUR RESPONSE _____

_____

_____

These are some places we loved to go to often—like schools, parks, beaches—when we were growing up.

MY RESPONSE _____

_____

_____

YOUR RESPONSE _____

_____

_____

These are places we traveled to often—like relatives' houses or favorite vacation spots we returned to again and again.

MY RESPONSE _____

_____

_____

_____

YOUR RESPONSE _____

_____

_____

These are other important places in our story as sisters—places we went to together.

MY RESPONSE _____

_____

_____

YOUR RESPONSE _____

_____

_____

PLAYING TOGETHER

AS KIDS, WE WERE ALWAYS UP TO SOMETHING. CHOREOGRAPHING DANCE ROUTINES IN THE BACKYARD, CREATING ELABORATE IMAGINARY WORLDS TOGETHER, GETTING INTO MOM'S MAKEUP DRAWER. RECORD THOSE MEMORIES HERE.

These are some of the things we did to entertain ourselves when we were kids:

MY RESPONSE _____

_____

_____

YOUR RESPONSE _____

_____

_____

These are some of the imaginary roles we took on when we were playing:

MY RESPONSE _____

_____

_____

YOUR RESPONSE _____

_____

_____

Sometimes we got these people involved in our games:

MY RESPONSE _____

_____

YOUR RESPONSE _____

Describe one of these games that you still remember now in detail.

MY RESPONSE _____

_____

_____

_____

_____

YOUR RESPONSE _____

_____

_____

_____

_____

Add a photo of the two of you at play, or describe some other activities that you

enjoyed doing together.

SHARED JOY

SOME OF THE HAPPIEST MOMENTS IN LIFE HAPPEN DURING BIRTHDAYS, HOLIDAYS, AND OTHER SPECIAL OCCASIONS. REMEMBER SOME OF THE HAPPY MOMENTS YOU SHARED HERE.

Here's a memory from one of *your* birthdays that I'll always remember:

MY RESPONSE

You were turning: _____ I was this old: _____

This is what I remember: _____

_____

_____

YOUR RESPONSE

You were turning: _____ I was this old: _____

This is what I remember: _____

_____

_____

The best birthday present you ever gave me was:

MY RESPONSE

Gift: _____

Why I love it so much: _____

_____

_____

YOUR RESPONSE

Gift: _____

Why I love it so much: _____

_____

_____

My favorite memory from a holiday we celebrated together was:

MY RESPONSE

Holiday: _____ Year: _____

My memory is: _____

_____

_____

_____

YOUR RESPONSE

Holiday: _____ Year: _____

My memory is: _____

_____

_____

_____

This was a truly memorable family vacation from when we were growing up:

MY RESPONSE _____

Where we went: _____

Who else was there: _____

Some things we did during that vacation were: _____

_____

_____

A memory from that vacation is: _____

_____

_____

_____

_____

YOUR RESPONSE

Where we went: _____

Who else was there: _____

Some things we did during that vacation are: _____

_____

_____

A memory from that vacation is: _____

_____

_____

_____

Add a photo from or describe another vacation we took together: _____

_____

_____

_____

_____

_____

_____

_____

_____

_____

IMPORTANT MOMENTS

EVENTS SHAPE US AND OUR RELATIONSHIPS, ESPECIALLY BIG LIFE EVENTS LIKE BIRTHS, DEATHS, MARRIAGES, AND MORE. HERE ARE MOMENTOUS OCCASIONS WE'VE EXPERIENCED TOGETHER.

Important event: _____

Date: _____

The event was for this person or these people: _____

_____

This moment was important because:

MY RESPONSE _____

YOUR RESPONSE _____

A memory I have about you from this event is:

MY RESPONSE _____

_____

YOUR RESPONSE _____

_____

Important event: _____

Date: _____

The event was for this person or these people: _____

_____

This moment was important because:

MY RESPONSE _____

_____

_____

_____

YOUR RESPONSE _____

_____

_____

_____

A memory I have from this event is:

MY RESPONSE _____

_____

_____

_____

YOUR RESPONSE _____

_____

_____

_____

ACCOMPLISHMENTS

My sister is my little star.

—Gigi Hadid

I was really proud of you when you accomplished:

MY RESPONSE _____

_____

_____

YOUR RESPONSE _____

_____

_____

Because:

MY RESPONSE _____

_____

YOUR RESPONSE _____

_____

Another time I was really happy for you was when you:

MY RESPONSE _____

_____

_____

_____

_____

YOUR RESPONSE _____

_____

_____

_____

_____

_____

Because:

MY RESPONSE _____

_____

_____

_____

YOUR RESPONSE _____

_____

_____

_____

PART THREE

Looking Ahead Together

ON THE HORIZON

The future is made of the same stuff as the present.

—Simone Weil

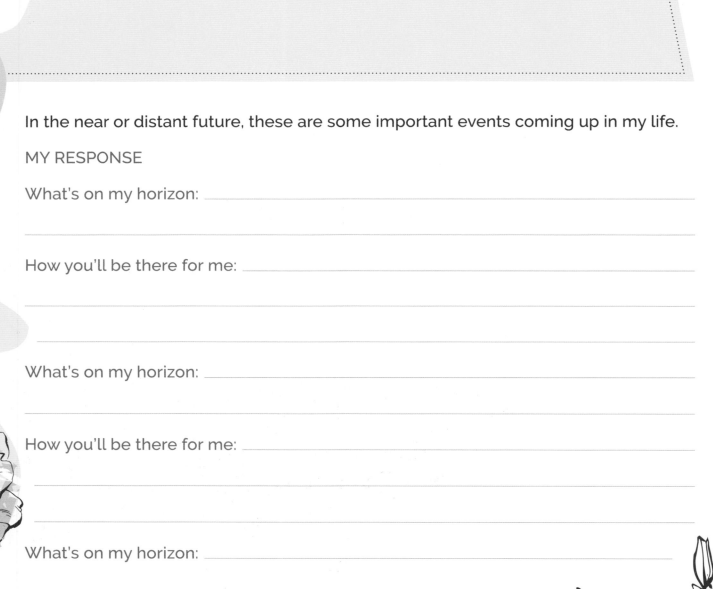

In the near or distant future, these are some important events coming up in my life.

MY RESPONSE

What's on my horizon: _____

_____

How you'll be there for me: _____

_____

_____

What's on my horizon: _____

_____

How you'll be there for me: _____

_____

_____

What's on my horizon: _____

_____

How you'll be there for me: _____

_____

YOUR RESPONSE

What's on my horizon: _____

_____

_____

How you'll be there for me: _____

_____

_____

_____

What's on my horizon: _____

_____

How you'll be there for me: _____

_____

_____

_____

What's on my horizon: _____

_____

_____

How you'll be there for me: _____

_____

_____

When I think about my future, I'm worried or anxious about these moments, and here's how I'll need your support.

MY RESPONSE

What's on my horizon: _____

_____

How you can support me: _____

_____

_____

What's on my horizon: _____

_____

How you can support me: _____

_____

_____

What's on my horizon: _____

_____

How you can support me: _____

_____

_____

_____

YOUR RESPONSE

What's on my horizon: _____
_____

How you can support me: _____
_____
_____
_____

What's on my horizon: _____
_____
_____

How you can support me: _____
_____
_____
_____

What's on my horizon: _____
_____

How you can support me: _____
_____
_____
_____

MAKING PLANS

If we could go on three perfect sister dates, they would be:

MY RESPONSE

1. _____

_____

2. _____

_____

3. _____

_____

YOUR RESPONSE

1. _____

_____

2. _____

_____

3. _____

_____

This is one of my favorite things we've done together, and I'd like to do it again.

MY RESPONSE

What we did: _____

_____

Why we should do it again: _____

_____

_____

_____

YOUR RESPONSE

What we did: _____

_____

Why we should do it again: _____

_____

_____

_____

Add a photo of or describe another favorite activity you did together.

Here's a place I'd like to travel to with you:

MY RESPONSE _____

Place: _____

This is why: _____

_____

_____

These are some of the things we could do there together: _____

_____

_____

_____

_____

_____

YOUR RESPONSE

Place: _____

This is why: _____

_____

_____

These are some of the things we could do there together: _____

_____

_____

_____

_____

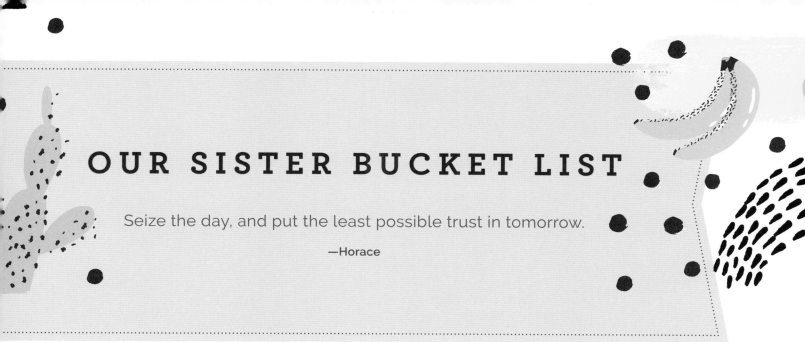

OUR SISTER BUCKET LIST

Seize the day, and put the least possible trust in tomorrow.

—Horace

HERE'S EVERYTHING WE HAVEN'T DONE YET, BUT WE WANT TO DO TOGETHER—NOW, SOON, OR IN THE FUTURE.

☐ _____

☐ _____

☐ _____

☐ _____

☐ _____

☐ _____

☐ _____

☐ _____

☐ _____

☐ _____

☐ _____

☐ _____

☐ _____

☐ _____

YOLO, SIS!

YOLO MEANS "YOU ONLY LIVE ONCE." CHALLENGE EACH OTHER TO DO SOMETHING THAT MIGHT BE A LITTLE AMBITIOUS OR NERVE-RACKING BUT COULD BE LIFE-CHANGING!

I dare you to: _____

_____

_____

YOUR RESPONSE _____

_____

_____

Challenge accepted? ☐ Yes! ☐ No way!

You dare me to: _____

_____

_____

MY RESPONSE _____

_____

_____

Challenge accepted? ☐ Yes! ☐ No way!

Double-dare! We dare *ourselves* to do this together: _____

_____

_____

_____

This was one time we went outside of our comfort zone together—and loved it!

Here's what we did: _____

_____

_____

_____

_____

_____

_____

FOR THE FOLLOWING PAGES, TALK TO EACH OTHER, BRAINSTORM TOGETHER, AND WRITE DOWN YOUR IDEAS.

The future is full of potential for creating new memories with your loved ones. Think about what you can make happen for your loved ones, using your sister powers. New traditions you could create, upcoming events you can turn into a big celebration, trips of a lifetime to honor your heritage, or even a dinner party with your family's favorite dishes—these are some activities we want to do together to create new memories with our family and the important people in our lives.

ACTIVITIES WE COULD DO, NEAR OR FAR . . .

Activity: _____

_____

_____

People we'd like to join us: _____

_____

Activity: _____

_____

_____

People we'd like to join us: _____

_____

Activity: _____

_____

_____

People we'd like to join us: _____

SISTERS, UNITE!

IS THERE A PROJECT YOU'VE ALWAYS WANTED TO TACKLE TOGETHER? A CAUSE THAT'S NEAR AND DEAR TO YOUR HEARTS? ARE THERE IMPORTANT PEOPLE IN YOUR LIVES THAT YOU WANT TO HONOR, TOGETHER? HERE ARE SOME WAYS WE CAN WORK TOGETHER FOR OTHERS.

A project we've always talked about doing together is: _____

_____

_____

This feels important or exciting to us because: _____

_____

_____

_____

Here's what we need to do to make this project a reality: _____

_____

_____

_____

A cause that we care about is: _____

_____

_____

Here are a few ideas for how we can get involved together: _____

_____

_____

These are people who have helped shape our lives as sisters—parents, grandparents, siblings, other relatives, neighbors, friends—and some ideas for things we can do together to celebrate or honor them:

Person: _____

What we could do: _____

_____

Person: _____

What we could do: _____

_____

Person: _____

What we could do: _____

_____

Person: _____

What we could do: _____

_____

Person: _____

What we could do: _____

_____

Person: _____

What we could do: _____

_____

Person: _____

What we could do: _____

_____

LOOKING BACK ON OUR STORY

PAGE BACK THROUGH THE RESPONSES YOU'VE WRITTEN IN THIS BOOK BEFORE ANSWERING THESE QUESTIONS.

What is the most surprising thing you've learned about your sister in these pages?

MY RESPONSE _____

_____

_____

YOUR RESPONSE _____

_____

_____

Is there something your sister wrote about you here that surprised you?

If so, how did that make you feel?

MY RESPONSE _____

_____

_____

YOUR RESPONSE _____

_____

_____

Is there something new that you learned about how you relate to your sister?

MY RESPONSE _____

_____

_____

YOUR RESPONSE _____

_____

HOPES AND THOUGHTS FOR THE FUTURE

Even in the future the story begins with Once Upon a Time.

—Marissa Meyer

My hopes for you are:

MY RESPONSE _____

_____

_____

_____

_____

_____

_____

_____

_____

_____

YOUR RESPONSE _____

_____

_____

_____

_____

_____

_____

_____

_____

_____

_____

_____

_____

_____

_____

_____

_____

My hopes for us are:

MY RESPONSE _____

_____

_____

_____

_____

_____

_____

_____

_____

_____

_____

_____

_____

_____

_____

_____

YOUR RESPONSE _____

_____

_____

_____

_____

_____

_____

_____

_____

_____

_____

_____

_____

_____

_____

_____

_____

_____

_____

If you're ever feeling unsure about yourself, remember this about who you are:

MY RESPONSE _____

_____

_____

_____

_____

_____

_____

_____

_____

_____

_____

_____

_____

_____

_____

YOUR RESPONSE

These are all the reasons why I feel so lucky to have you as my sister:

MY RESPONSE

YOUR RESPONSE _____

_____
_____
_____
_____
_____
_____
_____
_____
_____
_____
_____
_____
_____
_____
_____
_____
_____
_____
_____

OUR FAVORITE PHOTOS OF US TOGETHER

MY RESPONSE

This is my favorite photo of us. It was taken in _____ at _____
                                                    (year)   *(place)*

I love it because: _____

_____

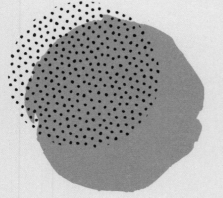

YOUR RESPONSE

This is my favorite photo of us. It was taken in _____ at _____
                                                    (year)   *(place)*

I love it because: _____

_____